STRANGE Suckers

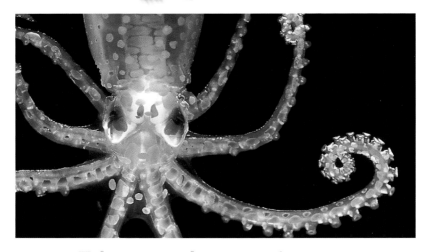

Take an underwater journey
to meet the cephalopods — the
strange suckers of the deep.

by Mark Norman

ETA® Cuisenaire

800-445-5985
www.etacuisenaire.com

Strange Suckers
ISBN 0-7406-4148-4
ETA 383091

ETA/Cuisenaire • Vernon Hills, IL 60061-1862
800-445-5985 • www.etacuisenaire.com

Series © 2006 by ETA/Cuisenaire®

Original version published by Nelson Australia Pty Limited (2002).
This edition is published by arrangement with Thomson Learning
Australia.

ETA/Cuisenaire
Manager of Product Development: Mary Watanabe
Creative Services Manager: Barry Daniel Petersen
Production Manager: Jeanette Pletsch
Lead Editor: Betty Hey
Copy Editor: Barbara Wrobel
Production Artist: Diana Chiropolos
Graphic Designer: Amy Endlich

Photographs by Mark Norman
Photographs on pp. i, ii, 3, 6, 10, 12, 16–17, 22, 27, and cover by
David Paul
Photograph on p. 8 courtesy of Museum of Natural History, Paris
Photograph on p. 27 courtesy of B. Reid

Teacher consultant: Garry Chapman, Ivanhoe Grammar School

Printed in China.

06 07 08 09 10 11 12 13 14 15   10 9 8 7 6 5 4 3 2 1

Contents

Chapter One

STRANGE Creatures

Some small squid hide in the sand during the day.

In our oceans live some strange animals called octopuses, squid, cuttlefish, and nautiluses [NAW-ti-luh-sez]. These creatures have big eyes, three hearts, and a brain the shape of a donut. And they can squirt ink.

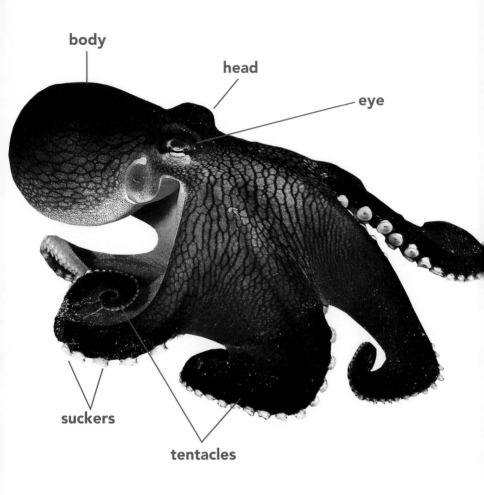

body

head

eye

suckers

tentacles

They are all cephalopods [SEF-a-la-pods]. <u>Cephalos</u> means "head" and <u>pod</u> means "foot." So a cephalopod's **tentacles**, or feet, come out of its head. A cephalopod's body includes its stomach, **gills**, and heart, which are stuck in a bag out the back.

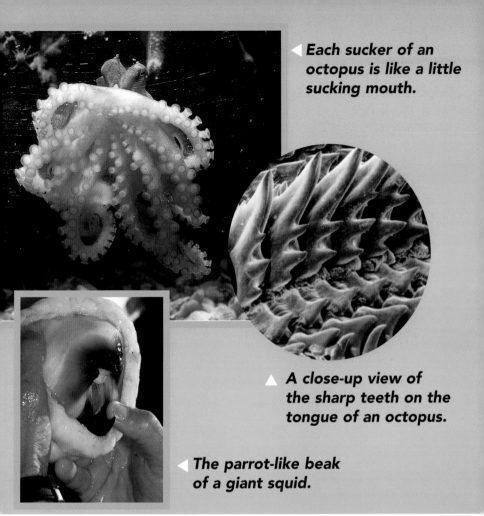

Each sucker of an octopus is like a little sucking mouth.

▲ *A close-up view of the sharp teeth on the tongue of an octopus.*

◄ *The parrot-like beak of a giant squid.*

On their tentacles, cephalopods have hundreds of **suckers**. These grab crabs and fish. At the base of the tentacles is the mouth. It has a large hard beak like a parrot's beak.

Inside the mouth, cephalopods have a special tongue covered in sharp teeth. It works like a chainsaw to tear up food.

▲ You can see the small dots of color on the skin of this cuttlefish.

This cuttlefish ▶ is pretending to be seaweed.

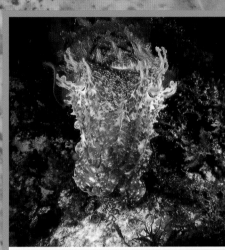

Cephalopods have amazing skin that can change color by turning millions of small colored dots on and off—just like a TV.

They can also push up spikes of skin to help them hide.

Chapter Two

Nautiluses

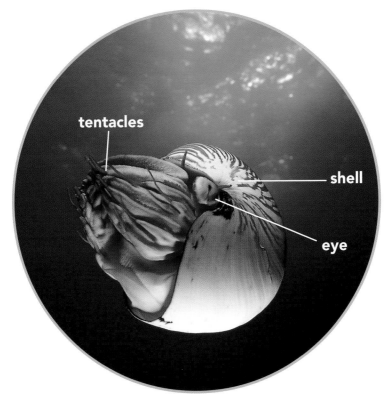

tentacles

shell

eye

The nautilus is the most **primitive** member of the cephalopods. It has a hard shell and 100 tentacles. If attacked, it can close a trapdoor and hide inside its shell.

This nautilus shell has been cut in half to show the space inside.

The shell of the nautilus has special features. Inside are lots of air spaces that help the animal float in the water. It would sink to the bottom of the deep sea without them.

Nautiluses live on the sides of coral reefs.
They hide in gangs in deep water during
the day. At night, they bob up to shallow
waters to feed on hermit crabs and dead
sea creatures.

Today, there are only six different types of nautiluses in the world. In the past, there were thousands. Some were the size of a van.

This fossil of a giant nautilus shell is in the Museum of Natural History, Paris, France. ▶

Chapter Three

Squid

Another member of this strange animal group is the squid. Most squid can swim fast and use fins to move around. They come in all different shapes and sizes.

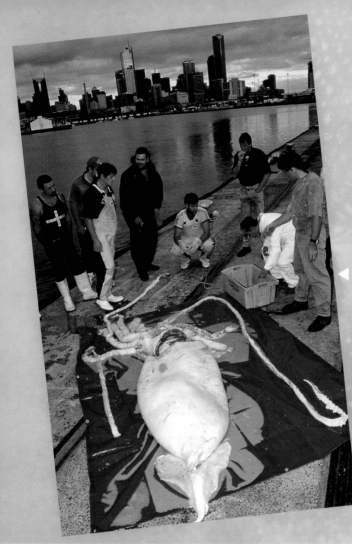

This giant squid was caught in the deep sea off the coast of Australia.

   Giant squid are the world's biggest invertebrates [in-VUR-te-brits]—animals that do not have a backbone. They can be as big as a bus—almost 60 feet long!

A scientist looking at the huge eye of a giant squid.

Giant squid live in the deep sea where it is always cold and dark. They have big eyes to see fish that give off light.

Sperm whales feed in the deep sea and are experts at catching and eating giant squid.

Squid can also
be very small.
Pygmy squid
are the smallest
squid in the
world. They
are tiny and
grow only to
the size of your
fingernail.

*Pygmy squid hold
on to seagrass
leaves using glue
from their skin.*

The dumpling squid is the size of a golf ball.

The dumpling squid is also small. During the day, it rakes sand over its head to hide. It comes out at night to hunt for shrimp and small fish.

13

The bright pattern of this squid warns fish that it is poisonous.

The striped pyjama squid is the king of slime. When this little squid is attacked, it squirts **poisonous** slime into the mouth of its attacker.

Chapter Four

Cuttlefish

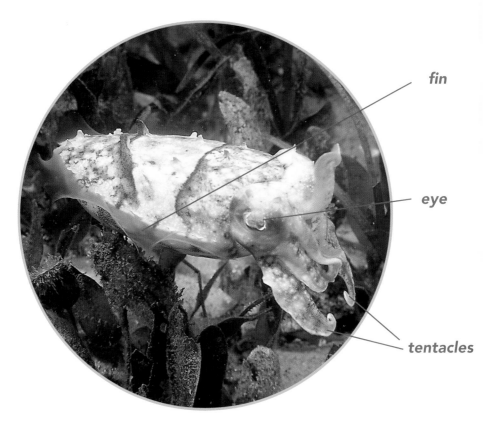

fin

eye

tentacles

Another group of strange suckers look like fat
squid. They are called cuttlefish. They are very
good at fast color changes.

The biggest cuttlebones grow up to 20 inches long.

You can sometimes see the marks from bird beaks and fish teeth in cuttlebones.

Cuttlefish have a special bone inside their bodies called a cuttlebone. It washes up on beaches after the animal dies. The cuttlebone contains hundreds of air layers that help the cuttlefish float in the water.

Dolphins sometimes leave teeth marks in cuttlebones.

Dolphins love eating cuttlefish. They search for them among the seaweed. When they catch one, they eat only the flesh, leaving the cuttlebone behind.

Cuttlefish use their color changes to do strange things. They seem to send secret signals to each other. Some can even **hypnotize** [HIP-ne-ties] their prey by changing color.

This cuttlefish is hiding in the sand.

This cuttlefish is pretending to be seaweed.

This cuttlefish looks like a leaf as it floats along in the current.

Cuttlefish are experts at hiding against different backgrounds. Some match sand, while others match seaweed. Some look like floating leaves.

Here, two male cuttlefish are trying to scare each other away.

At breeding time, male cuttlefish fight each other to impress the females. They do fast color changes and make themselves look as big as possible. If this does not work, they start biting each other.

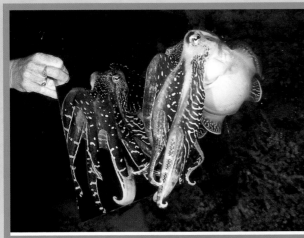

Here is a male cuttlefish trying to warn away his own reflection.

The cuttlefish becomes angry and tries to bite his reflection.

Male cuttlefish will even fight their own reflection in a mirror. When their warning display does not chase off the reflection, they start biting the mirror.

This flamboyant cuttlefish spends most of its time walking along the sea floor.

The flamboyant [flam-BOY-ant] cuttlefish is the most colorful species in the world. It is rare, and scientists do not know much about it. Its bright colors might be a sign that it is poisonous to eat.

Chapter Five

Octopuses

This octopus likes eating other octopuses.

Octopuses [OK-ta-puss-es] are sneaky. They are very good at hiding and squeezing through tiny holes. Because they have no shell, they can squeeze through holes about the size of their eye.

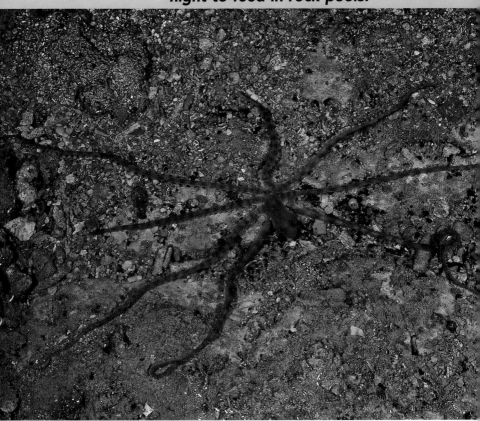

Some octopuses have very long arms. This is the string-arm octopus. If a fish attacks this octopus, it breaks off an arm. The fish eats the wriggling arm while the octopus sneaks away. The string-arm octopus then grows a new one.

24

People should always avoid touching small octopuses.

This is a deadly blue-ringed octopus. This small octopus has a poisonous bite that can kill humans. The blue rings of this octopus do not always show, but they do glow when the octopus gets angry.

The octopus known as a wunderpus lives in Indonesia and New Guinea.

This octopus has just been discovered by scientists. It is called a wunderpus. The bright colors probably mean it is poisonous.

The argonaut is one of the strangest octopuses. It spends its life swimming around in the open ocean. The female makes a beautiful shell and lives in it.

The white shells of female argonauts sometimes wash up on the beach.

The tiny male argonaut is the size of the female argonaut's eye. He has no shell and often hides among jellyfish.

After a closer look at these strange suckers, you might decide that cephalopods are not so strange after all.

Glossary

gills organs that help animals to breathe underwater

hypnotize [HIP-ne-ties] to send someone or something into a trance-like sleep

poisonous causes harm, or even death

primitive from an early age of the world

suckers parts of an animal that stick to an object by suction

tentacles long feelers used for touching and holding

Index